# Sandals:
## The Journey of Abraham and Sarah & Hagar

A Suite of Poems

by

James D. Rapp

# Dedication

Many sermons, Bible study classes, college courses, books and conversations are reflected in these poems. Authors like Robert Alter and C.S. Lewis, and teachers like T.J. Jones at North Central Bible College and Dr. Clyde Curry Smith at the University of Wisconsin – River Falls have shaped the way I see, and the respect with which I attempt to "handle" the Scriptures. My wife, Alice, has provided a marriage-worth of encouragement for more than half a century and tolerated the hours I spend in my office attempting to use my time creatively. Her keen eye has caught and corrected many errors that the "spell-checker" and I had missed. I must also acknowledge a debt to my career-long colleague and friend, Rick Grangaard, master of inventive names for his many pets, for the evocative one I chose to use in three of these poems, *Underfoot*. Thanks, Rick, for that and even more for the years of serious, and not so serious, conversation. Further, I owe credit to my sophomore high school English teacher, Winifred Rhodes, for defining poetry as, "the best use of the best words," thus giving me the hope that what I write rises at times to a level that deserves the name of poetry. But it would be akin to plagiarism to present these poems without acknowledging, with gratitude, the invaluable contributions of Cheryl Brandt. She has, over the years, read, discussed, and critiqued these poems. It is impossible to know now which ideas contained in the them came from her mind or which ones are now better stated because of her critique. Any errant interpretation or clumsiness in construction of these poems must, of course, be charged to my account, the result of an untrained amateur poet's stubborn insistence upon doing them his own way. To all of these who have contributed, knowingly or unknowingly, I say, "Thank you!" To you I dedicate this suite of poems.

# Introduction

The astonishing fact, discovered by those who look carefully into the past, is not how different it is from their own era but how many similarities there are. It is not as surprising, though, when one considers that there is a common element that holds all of human history, and indeed all of geological-galactical history, together. *We are all made of mud.* Paul, the Apostle of the Christian Church, said, in a different context, "We have this treasure in earthen vessels." Paul had a particular treasure in mind, and the mortal human body as its *earthen vessel*, but it is true that all treasure is housed in "earthen vessels", mere *mud*. The farthest galaxy and the smallest sub-particle of matter, with humankind standing somewhere between those extremes, share the same elemental ingredients brought into being by the creative command, "Let there be!" Reformed theology holds that God has spoken (is speaking) through His creation as well as through the recorded Scriptures. I would cautiously suggest that there is nothing that exists, whether of the physical universe or of the works and actions of mankind within and as a part of that universe, that is not revelatory of God. Even the most heinous of crimes, whether of man against man, or of mankind against "nature" testifies, through tragic contrast, to a "treasure" thus marred or lost.

So it is with a sense of the sacredness of *all creation* that I attempt to make my way through this world, knowing that every step I take treads on some treasure that has the potential to reveal God. All of my upbringing, my tradition of faith, and my personal faith teach me to respect the Word of God whether I find it in a microbe, in a sunrise, in a child's face, in a symphony, in a janitor's job well done – or in the pages of Holy Scripture.

Theologians debate, endlessly, about the origins and meanings of the Old and New Testaments. I don't find those debates uninteresting, nor do I lack opinions regarding the issues discussed. But in my role of poet I choose to look, without regard for matters of *inerrancy, infallibility, authorship, transmission*, etc., for *treasures* – glimmers at times, lightning flashes at other times – that are revelatory of God and his purposes for mankind. The Bible, thick book that it is, is curiously stingy at times with the details it gives us, skipping whole decades without a word, falling silent for hundreds of years, naming some characters we have little interest in knowing and letting others who are central to the story pass by unnamed. I can't say why I love such an "unfulfilling" book, except to say that I find in it *treasures in earthen vessels* that captivate me, haunt my imagination, and inspire me to believe in its God.

Abraham and Sarah – and Hagar – are recognizable because they are made of that same *mud* that we are made of. They are *treasures in earthen vessels* that reveal the unending struggle of mankind to connect – or re-connect – with their Maker and make sense of His purpose for their lives. We know too little about Abraham and Sarah to write their biography but we know enough about them to consider them treasures. The poems in this book are not biographical; many of them are pure fiction. We know nothing of the early life of Abram and Sarai, nothing of their courtship and marriage, and whole decades of their life together are skipped over by the Biblical record. I am indebted to Robert Alter for pointing out that, at the end of their lives, after the near sacrifice of Isaac, Abraham and Sarah appear to have lived apart from each other, requiring Abraham, upon hearing of Sarah's death, to make a journey of two or more days to mourn for her and bury her. But my speculation that such a separation was the result of estrangement is just that, a speculation.

So these poems are not offered as a theological exposition of Genesis, chapters 11 through 25. I do attempt, in those poems that commemorate known incidents in the life of Abraham, to understand the implications of those events for his faith, and for the faith of all the sons and daughters of Abraham who have drawn hope and inspiration from them. But even in those cases I may have failed in my attempt to find their original meaning and import. What I hope I have succeeded in doing is to present a picture, not uncommon in our own day, of men and women, *mud*-men and *mud*-women, who nonetheless were created by God, treasured by God, visited by God, and approved by God for their (imperfect) obedience to his calling.

It is a wonderful experience, a life-affirming experience, to see sandal prints in ancient sand. They let us know that some other *mud*-son or *mud*-daughter has walked this way before us.

## Contents

Sarai ...................................................................... 1

Underfoot ............................................................. 2

Sandals .................................................................. 3

Changes ................................................................ 5

Revelation ............................................................. 7

Maiden Prayer ...................................................... 9

Abram's Decision ............................................... 11

The Proposal ...................................................... 13

Sarai's Decision ................................................. 14

Sarai's Wedding Day ......................................... 16

Looking Two Ways ............................................ 18

Sarai In A New Land .......................................... 20

The First Quarrel ............................................... 22

Springtime .......................................................... 24

The Altars of Abraham ...................................... 25

Melchizedek ....................................................... 27

After the Rescue of Lot ..................................... 29

Hagar On The Run ............................................. 32

| | |
|---|---|
| Circumcision | 33 |
| A Well Planned Encounter | 34 |
| The Road To Zoar | 37 |
| Sarai In Abimelech's Harem | 38 |
| Unintended Consequences | 42 |
| The Voice of God | 47 |
| On The Mountain | 49 |
| At Kiriath Arba | 51 |
| An Old Woman Remembers (Hagar's Recompense) | 53 |
| Abraham at Sarah's Tomb | 55 |
| The Burial of Abraham | 58 |
| A Complicated Faith | 60 |
| A One-way Conversation With God | 62 |
| Afterword | 65 |
| Alphabetical List of Poems | 77 |

*Sandals: The Journey of Abraham and Sarah & Hagar*

Sarai
(From half–brother, Abram at ten years old)

Sarai, tiny desert rose,
Half an arm's length, head to toes.
Father's child — sister half,
Mother's blood has launched your craft.

Sarai, *princess — queen*
With no kingdom to be seen;
No attendant waits to serve and bow;
To nurse, a breast you borrow now.

Sarai, sister–part,
Tiny hands that seize my heart,
Tiny fingers, feet, and toes —
Going where, God only knows.

*Sandals: The Journey of Abraham and Sarah & Hagar*

Underfoot
(From fifteen year old Abram to five-year-old Sarai)


Oh, Underfoot! You are wounded again,
And because of my forgetfulness.
Come, let me see the wound, and hold it —
Bathe it gently in the balm of my regretfulness.

Sit here, on my lap. . . your curls upon my shoulder,
My shirt receives your tears;
The tenderness of cheek-on-cheek heals *me*,
And lifts the sense of blame I bear.

How many times, dear bleeding one
Have those poor feet been trodden on
And your dear gladness shattered suddenly
By my unthinking turn?

You must remember, sister–child,
That I have things to think about and do,
And if you choose to follow close to me
My steps could bring great harm to you.

I also am an Underfoot, dear child –
I follow close, Yahweh God, and quickly turn to go His way,
So if you choose to follow close to me, just know —
My steps may wound your heart some day.

*Sandals: The Journey of Abraham and Sarah & Hagar*

Sandals
(From twenty–one year–old Abram)


I cannot walk the desert without my sandals.
The heat will blister my feet.
And I cannot be expected to handle
The impish impertinence I always meet
When you, little friend,
Decide to torment me with pranks
That will never end.

Sarai, you have two lovely sandals to wear.
You walk on pavement of stone
On a broad well traveled thoroughfare;
You need no sandals except your own.
Have pity then
On your brother whose feet tread desert sand,
Whose sandals are worn thin.

Ah, there they are, it wasn't you who hid them from me.
But you smile — you laugh as though you,
And not Yahweh, planned the test to see
Whom I would blame, to see what I would do.
Sarai, little one,
You must know that God is always testing us;
The tests are never done.

*Sandals: The Journey of Abraham and Sarah & Hagar*

Someday, dear Sarai, your tests will come.
Sarai — "princess", now, we call you —
But that name will seem a mockery when from
This settled home you're called to move.
Sandals sturdy then
You'll need, and spirit even sturdier to bear the strain
Of wills worn thin.

*Sandals: The Journey of Abraham and Sarah & Hagar*

Changes
(Sarai at 13, Abram at 23)

Sarai, the months away have changed you so . . .
The little bird whose former love
Took form of kisses, hugs, and teases –
Hours upon my lap and in my arms –
Stands now, shyly by – she does not know
If she should fly into my arms . . . poor bashful dove.

Sister–half, I've always loved you whole,
Arms full – an undivided love – the truest kind;
Loved you – loved loving you –
And loved the love you gave to me.
But now, sister–shy, I sense the thoughts that darkly stole
Into your heart to cloud your mind.

Sister–child, I have hurt you once again;
My offenses spread like desert weeds.
My months away seemed a betrayal mean,
Of our friendship; they have sown the seeds
That now bear fruit of coldness. And now you strain
To keep your balance – waver like bird upon a reed.

Ah, my child, how can I help you understand
The Necessity that drives me from you?
From you? Yes . . . but also draws us hand in hand
For some hidden purpose . . . to some mission new.
Sarai, has our love become – for you – a chaffing prison band –
A cuff of iron for each of us – and chain between the two?

*Sandals: The Journey of Abraham and Sarah & Hagar*

Father's child, I have been away these months,
Not, this time, on father's business,
But exploring, instead, the lonely labyrinths
Of Yahweh's austere Father–ness;
Sitting long to hear His voice beneath the terebinths;
Learning love that asks for all I have, no less.

The change you see is cause, you think, for wariness.
Cause it is, my Sister–friend, for wariness, and for caution.
This Yahweh – Father God – asks nothing less
Than all one has to give, and will accept no ration
Of one's loyalty; no division of, no adding too, no stinginess.
A life of total abnegation.

But you are changing too, shy desert floret.
More woman now, than child I see –
Child–gem become a lovely woman–aigrette.
And I, seeing, feel a shyness coming over me.
Still sister–friend, still sister–child, and yet
Apart now – apart, and wondering what will be.

*Sandals: The Journey of Abraham and Sarah & Hagar*

    Revelation
  (Sarai at 14, Abram at 24)

Sarai, come! Sister! Friend!
Come near.
It is time to talk again.
The weeks have passed since I've returned
And still we're "edging 'round each other" –
Wondering if the flame that once had burned
So brightly, has gone out altogether.

Sarai, listen! Come! Sit near!
Don't be shy.
I am not angry with you, dear.
I need to tell you what is in my heart
That makes me seem, sometimes, severe;
Things you see that make you stand apart,
Afraid to know this brother–friend, austere.

Thank you, Sarai. Sit there,
At my feet if you wish;
My knees – a prop – will gladly bear
Your arms and chin and make a path
Straight into your eyes and heart.
You smile now, and cannot know the half
Of how that fills my every living part.

My every living part!
My very soul!
You've claimed me from the start,
Sister–friend; from an infant in my arms
You've grown to be a . . .
A princess with the beauty, grace, and charms
I see in you today.

*Sandals: The Journey of Abraham and Sarah & Hagar*

Sarai, "Queen of Ur"!
I am not alone
In seeing the ardor
Of every young man who passes by.
Your father Terah has made me vow
To keep his daughter – princess shy –
As safe through life as now.

And Yahweh . . . oh Sarai, dear,
Do not grow cold!
Feel how His warmth is near!
He is a fire in me, and wants to warm you too.
He has plans for me I want to tell you of –
You need to hear His plans; His plans for you.
Don't leave! Please stay and hear, my frightened Dove.

Sit again, Sarai . . . don't go away!
Don't go!
We'll talk of other things today,
And on another, when your heart is stronger,
And your will less strong,
You'll find that you can bear much longer
Things that now you think are wrong.

*Sandals: The Journey of Abraham and Sarah & Hagar*

Maiden Prayer
(Sarai's First Prayer to Yahweh at Age 16)

Yahweh – God of Abram – hear me!
Yahweh, whom I know not – whose face I cannot see;
Yahweh God, unlike the gods of Ur
Whose presence seems so sure;
Gods of wood and stone – homely gods
With roots, like mine, in earthly sod.

Abram says he speaks to you
And hears you tell him what to do.
He says the gods of Ur are not Gods at all;
Cannot see their people's need, nor hear their call.
But you, he says, can hear and see.
And so, my fervent prayer, "Yahweh, answer me!"

Answer me, God of Abram . . .
Or do you only talk to men?
Some men came the other day
And Abram stopped them in the way,
And when the day was done I heard him say,
"The Angel of Yahweh, and His hosts, have come my way."

Are there no angels who will speak to me?
Is there no sound of you; no thing that I can see?
The gods of Ur are made of silent rock and clay,
But holy men of Ur can tell you what they say.
Abram will not tell me what you say to me,
And what he says you say to him, I pray will never be.

*Sandals: The Journey of Abraham and Sarah & Hagar*

He says you call him to a foreign place – a place
Where you will plant a nation, birth a race.
And though it would be hard enough to see him go,
He says that *I*, and *Father Terah*, and *Lot* must go also.
Are we to leave a settled land, and pilgrims then become;
Servants of a silent, unseen God, with neither land nor home?

I'm asking you to hear me, Yahweh, Abram's Choice!
But what I really want is to hear that same voice
That Abram hears – to know the God he knows.
To have you tell *me* why it is that *I* must go;
To speak to *me*, as you speak to *him*, in ways that *I* can hear;
In ways that tell me things I need to know to calm my growing fear.

Yahweh – God of Abram – answer me!

*Sandals: The Journey of Abraham and Sarah & Hagar*

### Abram's Decision

Yahweh God – You know your servant well;
Know that he will follow you beyond the farthest tel.
But you complicate your servant's task
By insisting that he do exactly as you ask
Regarding these recalcitrants whose
Necks you wish to save from an Urugatic noose.

Lot you would save, though he little cares for you;
A decent lad, himself, but too absorbed in – to determined to pursue –
The good things of a settled life:
Solid walls to ward off strife,
A place at the gate, and a pretty Urugatic wife.
He picks his gods with calculating eye and shares the loyalties
That should be yours, with Urugatic deities.

Terah – father Terah – who should know you well
Stumbles over terra cotta gods and tries to quell
The nagging thoughts that come each night to tell
Him he has sacrificed his sons and daughters . . . and two wives as well
To this Urugatic prison – this god–factory – this empty, god–less shell;
Building shrines to please his kin, though he knows full well
That you are God alone . . . that in your halls no stone nor clay can dwell.

And Sarai – tender Sarai – friend of Abram's heart –
Cannot understand why you would have us part
With all the "beauty" of these Urugatic avenues,
Tree–line thoroughfares, where daily, travelers bring the news
Of wonders to be known, and hawk their wares of silken grace.
I see her hold them to her lovely face,
Imagining a princess in a noble Urugatic place.

*Sandals: The Journey of Abraham and Sarah & Hagar*

And I, Yahweh God, am little better than the rest.
I've struggled with you – told you I'm unequal to the test;
Told you that I stumble when I cannot see the path.
But then you thunder in my mind and I know your wrath
Will soon engulf this Urugatic cesspool, and I know
That I must gather those you've called to go,
And take them with me – with their will, or no.

*Sandals: The Journey of Abraham and Sarah & Hagar*

### The Proposal

It isn't really "news" to me,
I've known for weeks now,
Since Abram came to see
Our Father Terah, asking how —
Or if — a brother–half could be
Allowed to "tie" to matrimony's plow,
His sister–half, and wondering if she
Would gladly take such vow.

I should be honored that I'm "asked."
My friends have all been "given" away;
Sent by fathers – carried by near–strangers – to new tasks,
Changed to wives, from children, in a day.
Abram's choice I'd be at last;
Abram's wife, with whom, as child, he used to play;
Once sister; now as sister–bride re–cast,
To serve and follow him always.

To learn to love him, we are told,
Is the bride's first service, a task
I've worked upon, and mastered from of old;
The love I show to Abram is no mere mask –
I've loved him from the very start.
Before my lips could clearly speak his name
My eyes and hands and heart
Had memorized his frame.

And so your choice of me, brother, Abram–dear,
Confirms my choice of you,
Made daily in my heart through every passing year;
A choice to love you as a sister true.
And now you've chosen me – as bride –
And wait to know our Father Terah's will;
You wait and wonder, trying hard to hide
The fear that Terah's "No" will leave me then, a sister still.

*Sandals: The Journey of Abraham and Sarah & Hagar*

Sarai's Decision

My friends say he is old,
But I am not, my self, young now.
It is many years since I was told
Where I could go, and when, and how.

And besides, father Terah says
That Abram's age will honor me –
That waiting for me all these days
Is tribute to the precious gift in me he sees.

My love for Abram
Was my first conscious thought,
But as a ewe, submitting to a ram? . . .
That is not the kind of love I sought.

I loved him as a brother dear
Who chased me, caught me, hugged me,
Kissed me . . . held me near.
But . . . as husband? Oh, Yahweh, can it be?

Oh Yahweh, It is you,
Not Abram that I fear.
Abram's only wish is that he do
Your will and feel you near.

Abram loves you more than any *thing*;
More than life – his life, or any life, I know;
Houses, lands, wife and child he'd fling
Into the night if you would tell him to.

## *Sandals: The Journey of Abraham and Sarah & Hagar*

Am I to be a bride to such as he?
He says you've promised him a family;
A nation of great size and dignity;
A nation of great worth to Thee.

Oh Yahweh, If I could hear your voice,
And know without a doubt that it is true,
And that to love this man would be a choice
That I'd not later rue,

Then Yahweh – Abram's God –
I'd go with gladness, live in tents,
Forsaking houses made of sod,
And never rue the loss of Ur's accouterments.

But you give me no guarantee –
Nothing I can hold, or hear or see –
Only Abram's word that you will cause to be
A nation great, that comes from me.

I go, Yahweh, Abram's God . . .
I go, for love of Abram, and of Father Terah too.
I go for love of kindred blood.
In trust of Abram's trust, I go – through him in trust of You.

*Sandals: The Journey of Abraham and Sarah & Hagar*

### Sarai's Wedding Day

He is my husband now, and I his wife.
A simple pledge, a few brief words,
A night of banqueting, and now my life
Is redirected Abram–ward.

He is my husband now, my recent friend.
How are we to make this change?
Must all the old ways end
And be replaced with something strange?

How will a brother, friend of my childhood heart,
Now become my lover?
Will his arms still play the brother's part
Of comforter and cover?

Or will they only draw me to his chamber
When *he* wills to have me there,
Only offer me his favor
When he's seeking for an heir?

He is my husband now, my lord;
His will is my will, his plans my goal,
His destiny a many-stranded cord
That I am bound to, heart and soul.

He is my husband now, and I his wife –
I who used to hide his sandals,
Tease and pester him with friendly strife,
Causing him to cry out, "Vandals!" –

*Sandals: The Journey of Abraham and Sarah & Hagar*

I am now his wife, and feel the difference
As he takes me in his arms.
An embrace that only *gave* before, is now, I sense,
A drawing in, a drinking from my charms.

This pledge I've made leaves no defense
Against a husband–lover's claims,
Nor am I sure the things in him I sense,
Are any different from my aims.

But as Abram's wife must I forego
The sweet joy of sister–love
To learn a way I do not know,
Trade away my brother–trove?

How does a sister, once friend of Abram's heart,
Become his lover, help–mate, spouse?
The change required I know will start
By sharing Abram's body, faith, and house.

Oh, Yahweh, Abram's God,
Think not that I your gifts dismiss,
And please, Lord, think it not so odd
That I should weep on such a day as this.

*Sandals: The Journey of Abraham and Sarah & Hagar*

    Looking Two Ways
   (Abram & Sarai Leaving Ur)

   They are loaded now, twenty camels strong.
   I had guessed ten, but it is clear that I was wrong.
   Sarai, with her clearer eye could easily see
   What I could not; things not visible to me.

They are empty now, bare rooms awaiting dust,
Or perhaps a bride and her man in whom she puts her trust.
They'll build a walled world of safety where no shaft can thrust
To disturb them, or lure them with vain wanderlust.

   Morning is near, Yahweh, my loved;
   At last, the journey awaited, that you've told me of;
   At last, the dust of Ur to be shaken away,
   To be only a memory at the end of the day.

Sunrise, Yahweh God, on a day I prayed would never be,
Casting shadows on my heart and every *thing* I see;
On every *thing* I've owned and cared for lovingly;
On the fearless, awe–full, man you gave to me.

See him stand with back to sun,
As though he'd lead it, as he journeys on
To his promised home, and make it there,
A token of his Yahweh's favor fair.

As though he'd rob this world of all that's bright,
Taking with him camel–loads of precious freight;
Taking those you've said must go;
Leaving only "dust" for wind to blow.

*Sandals: The Journey of Abraham and Sarah & Hagar*

    Yahweh God, I cannot see beyond the next rise,
    But I shall walk in the light of your sun–lit skies;
    Walk even in darkness, knowing that there
    Your sun is coming to make things clear.

    And wherever you lead me, or cause me to go;
    Wherever I hear your voice, or see you, or know
    Your presence has been – there, Yahweh God, I'll raise
    An altar to you, a "sun", a "light", to speak your praise.

Farewell to streets well known and loved,
To cool water in a river that flowed,
To friends, foods, songs, fields, and houses dear.
Farewell — I'll remember you, and wish you near.

Oh home! At just the moment I had hoped to see –
To catch a final, loving glimpse, to be
My last, and lasting memory –
The blinding sun came up obscuring you from me.

    I see your light, Yahweh God, on yonder hill,
    A beacon pointing to your sacred will.
    Ask any earthly thing; assign any earthly task;
    For the joy of that light, I'll do what you ask.

    All I have is yours, Yahweh God, twenty camels strong;
    Men, and beasts, and things, to you belong.
    All I need is you – to hear your voice, Yahweh God –
    And not an inch, will I require, of earthly sod.

*Sandals: The Journey of Abraham and Sarah & Hagar*

### Sarai In A New Land

The differences, you ask?
The things I see, and the tasks
I must do, are all new . . .
From my rising until the day is through.

It's true, I've been relieved of rooms to clean –
Goat skin tents are all I've seen
Since leaving Ur,
Except for cities from afar.

But it is not as though there is nothing now to do;
The tent . . . Ah! A tent will always need more than a few
Stitches here and there, and I'm expected to
Keep it in repair . . . Abram's words are , "Like new!"

And there are meals to prepare;
Morning and evening I stare
At my meager "kitchen" and remember where
Once I enjoyed more lavish fare.

The land? . . . Abram says it will be ours,
But it isn't like "ours" used to be, with towers
To heaven, and fields ringed with flowers . . .
With shaded paths to walk for hours on hours.

This land . . . towers above us, capped with snow,
And plummets to depths that are far below,
With paths where only the sure–footed ibexes go;
A land where nothing but wild things grow.

*Sandals: The Journey of Abraham and Sarah & Hagar*

The differences, you want to know?
I think of all the things that I've let go
The one I miss the most of all
Is the secretness of a solid wall.

Our days, once privated in gardens, walled,
Are open now, their good and bad exposed to all;
The quiet breeze conspires to steal my lonely call;
I dare not even let a tearful whisper fall.

I dare not speak the things I feel most keen,
Lest others hear and thus it seem
That some divide has come between
Us – Abram and his "princess–queen."

And I, within my tent, can hear the things
Discussed – the words that pass between
The women . . . I have heard and seen
Them talk of "Abram's barren princess–queen."

*Sandals: The Journey of Abraham and Sarah & Hagar*

### The First Quarrel

We have not quarreled much,
We have loved too much for that.
Oh, of course we've wounded such
That . . . Well, I remember days when I have sat
In stubborn silence, or when Abram
Found a need to go away;
Days when we have turned our backs, or ran
Into ourselves instead of stay
And say the thing that brought our anger on.

But today I stayed . . .
And Abram stayed . . .
I began with anger and ended with tears.
He started defensive, expressing his fears.
It was all about teraphim, small clay idols
I'd brought in the stuff from Ur to console
Me for the loss of my homeland.
With one grand sweep of his hand
Abram destroyed them, reduced them to sand;
All that is left is this dust in my hand.

This dust, and the anger that burned
At the man whose love of Yahweh caused him to spurn
All things dear to my heart;
Home and kin and . . . and familiar hearth,
Everything . . . here on this earth,
Everyone is sacrificed so that he may earn
Some promise . . . some . . . some
Far–away promise of many sons.

*Sandals: The Journey of Abraham and Sarah & Hagar*

Abram cursed the teraphim,
Ground them under his heel,
As if his words and actions
Could somehow seal
Off his world and make it immune
To the evils he sees at each turn.
And I wept as I swept the dust
Of my gods into my hand . . .

Abram walks with confidence in this strange land,
Talking, and listening to Yahweh's command;
I have nothing . . . nothing but losses . . . and
Here in my hand . . . nothing but tears and sand.

*Sandals: The Journey of Abraham and Sarah & Hagar*

    Springtime

Springtime is the hardest time.
I see the calving cows and lambing ewes.
And all year long
I watch the servants' quarters grow . . .
The years are passing by, I know . . .
And with them hope . . .
And with them hope . . .
Each year more precious hope will go.

Abram, faithful Abram,
Comes to my bed with hope
Inspired by visions, dreams or voices . . .
I do not know, I cannot know.
I only know I welcome him because he hopes.
I welcome him because I hope with him
For just a little while, until, again I know . . .
Until, again, the bitter truth I know.

Abram, faithful Abram,
Could be like other men,
Could be like bulls or rams
Who build a harem
So every seed will find a fertile nest.
But Abram, trusting God,
Has chosen not to go that way.
Each day he comes to me alone
And draws my hopeless heart
Into his hoping breast.
And there, for just a little while
My hopeless heart finds rest.

*Sandals: The Journey of Abraham and Sarah & Hagar*

The Altars of Abraham

These altars!
Piles of river rock!
I could laugh at them
If Abram didn't take such stock,
Such joy in making them;
Built at cost of bruises,
Aches and pains;
Bending, lifting,
Bending once again
Until a tiny ziggurat arose.
And then upon its humble height,
He, his offering lays.

I remember well the days
When Abram, gazed
Upon the ziggurat of Ur
And swore that he no more
Would worship stone or clay,
But make them servants
Of his God someday;
Give them voice
And make them say
The things all men should say
In praise of his Yahweh.

*Sandals: The Journey of Abraham and Sarah & Hagar*

And there he lays his gift;
A lamb before his God, he lays;
His finest lamb!
And then he prays.
I cannot bear to hear his prayers.
They tear a part of me away
As though . . . as though
A part of me he'd freely give away.

Oh Yahweh, God of Abram, stern!
Do you demand what he,
In prayer is offering you?
Is there nothing Abram has
That Your consuming fire
Would not receive and burn?

*Sandals: The Journey of Abraham and Sarah & Hagar*

    Melchizedek
    (Genesis 14:17-24)

Melchizedek, model, mentor,
    mediator, magistrate,
    monarch? Mostly mystery.

Melchizedek, King of Salem,
Priest of *El Elyon*, God Most High,
Bearer of bread and wine
To victorious Abram;
Blessing Abram in the name
Of his unnamed God;
Blessing his unnamed God
For victorious Abram;
Receiving tithe from Abram –
A tenth of Sodom's reclaimed wealth.

The king of Salem served a God
He could not name, except to call him,
"God Most High,
Creator of heaven and earth."
The heavens and the earth –
Creations of His hand –
Had made it plain that over all
There stood an unnamed One
To Whom all other claimants
To the name of "god" must bow.

*Sandals: The Journey of Abraham and Sarah & Hagar*

Abram, missionary, evangelist,
To this benighted world,
Could name the God, Most High.
When tempted by Sodom's King
To enrich himself with Sodom's
Reclaimed "goods" He said,
"I have raised my hand
To *Yahweh, El Elyon,*
Creator of heaven and earth,
And sworn an oath that I will take,
Not a thread, nor a sandal,
So that you can never say,
"By the wealth of Sodom's "goods"
Abram was made rich."

*Sandals: The Journey of Abraham and Sarah & Hagar*

After The Rescue of Lot
(Genesis 15)

Even men of faith have doubts and fears.
Abram believed God, no doubt,
But was his God–pleasing faith
Not sometimes mixed with doubt and fear?

Was Abram bold and fearless
As he marched his little army
Out to meet the Kings who captured Lot,
Looted Sodom and Gomorrah?

Troublesome Lot had forced his hand,
Made him visible in the land,
Made him vulnerable should the kings
Regroup and seek revenge.

Yahweh, sensing Abram's fears, came to him:
"Do not be afraid," He said;
"I am your shield,
Your very great reward."

"Shield? I am your shield?"
Small comfort to a man,
Wandering in a strange land,
Too weak to claim a single foot of soil.

"Very great reward?" Bitter words
To an ancient childless man
Whose only heir was Eliezer, a servant
Whose very name mocked reality.

*Sandals: The Journey of Abraham and Sarah & Hagar*

But *Eliezer*, the *God who helps*, drew near:
"Look up at the heavens and count the stars!
Go ahead, see if you can count them.
So, your descendants shall be."

So Abram, ceased to count his fears,
Looked up, believed God, pleased God,
And his faith was credited to him
As righteousness.

"Abram, I called you out of Ur of Chaldea
To give you this land as an inheritance."
"How can I know, Sovereign Yahweh,
That I will gain possession of it?"

"Bring me a heifer, Abram,
A goat and ram, each three years old;
A dove and a pigeon too.
Prepare to cut a covenant with me."

The old man moved with practiced skill,
Each creature slain and halved;
One half laid to the right,
One half laid to the left.

When birds of prey descended on the parts
The old man drove them off, defending them,
Preserving them in their helplessness,
Till Yahweh came and drove the birds away.

*Sandals: The Journey of Abraham and Sarah & Hagar*

In a deep sleep, as the sun was setting –
In a thick and dreadful darkness
The old man lay, exhausted from his labors.
Yahweh drew near and spoke:

"Your children will be prey in a strange land,
Enslaved and mistreated for hundreds of years.
But I will save them from their predators
And bring them back to inhabit this land."

At sunset a blazing, smoking torch appeared
And made its way between the pieces,
And Yahweh swore a covenant with Abram,
"To your descendents I give this land."

In the trail of smoke dim shapes appeared
That Abram could not know nor name:
Abram's Sons in grand procession;
Isaac's sons, and Jacob's sons,

And last, as countless as the stars above,
Came hosts from every tribe and tongue,
The heirs of Abram's promise,
The sons of David's Son.

*Sandals: The Journey of Abraham and Sarah & Hagar*

Hagar on the Run
(Genesis 16)

I didn't ask to be a slave.
Who would ask to be a slave?
I didn't ask to be sent away
As "maidservant," in the entourage
Of a foreign woman I'd never known.

I didn't ask to be a surrogate
For a Hebrew woman
Desperate to have a son;
To be "given" to her man to raise up one
That *she* could call *her own*.

I didn't ask to lie alone tonight,
Sheltered, by the darkness,
From Sarai's tongue and lash,
Sheltering, in my body,
One for whom I didn't ask.

But you have found me, God who sees,
And tell me I must cease to run from Sarai's tongue,
Must turn again and bear *for Abram*, Ishmael, his son.
And you promise *me* unnumbered "sons"
Although I didn't ask for even one.

Because you sought me, God who sees,
I return to be, for Abram, a bearer of *his* seed.
You promised, and Your promise I believe,
That the son I didn't ask for, nonetheless will be
A child of Abram, co–inheritor with Abram's seed.

*Sandals: The Journey of Abraham and Sarah & Hagar*

### Circumcision
### (Genesis 17)

"Mark them, Abraham, as I have marked you."
When Abram was ninety-nine Yahweh came to him,
Changed his name, and Sarai's name,
Denoting greater changes yet to come,
Unborn nations yet to rise,
Inheritors of Abraham's promise,
Bearers of the Name of Abram's God.

Abraham must have wondered,
"Does Yahweh ever make a demand
Easy to respond to, easy to fulfill?"
It was beyond conception that,
At ninety-nine, he would father a child
By Sarah, who at eighty-nine,
Had long deserted hope of motherhood.

And what of this demand to mark himself,
And all the males who were his own,
As Yahweh's sons, by circumcision?
One thing was sure,
It left no time for hesitation
If he were going to heal in time
To do his part – God always leaves
A part for man to do.

So Abraham assembled all his men,
Including Ishmael, his son,
And on a single day,
A day of pain and blood,
Marked a race as Yahweh's sons;
Descendants of His servant, Abraham;
Inheritors, through him, of Canaan Land;
Progenitors, with him, of Yahweh's promise.

*Sandals: The Journey of Abraham and Sarah & Hagar*

## A Well Planned Encounter
### (Genesis 18)

What kind of man is it whom Yahweh Himself
Must consult before He executes his plan?
"Shall I hide from Abraham what I am about to do;
Abraham through whom all nations will be blessed?"

What kind of man is it who dares insert himself
Between Yahweh's sure and awful plan
And those deserving of the things He plans to do?
Only one through whom all nations will be blessed.

Did Abraham, who knew his God so well –
Had often called on Him by name –
Not know that it was He who walked with him?
Or did he try to feign forgetfulness?

No, Abraham, friend of God, knew full well.
And though he chose to use another name,
*Adonai*, my Lord, in addressing Him,
It was not because of his forgetfulness.

Cries had come to Yahweh concerning Sodom's sins;
Brutality engulfing young and old alike;
Masculinity expressed as incivility to strangers;
Incivility expressed in emasculation of real men.

Yahweh had come to ascertain the truth of Sodom's sins,
Wishing not to punish good and bad alike,
Assuming, for the journey, the guise of a stranger,
Taking upon Himself the form of ordinary men.

Who had cried to God concerning Sodom's sins,
A cry so great it prompted Him

*Sandals: The Journey of Abraham and Sarah & Hagar*

To go and see, to judge first hand,
The depths to which their sins had carried them?

Surely not Lot, who long had tolerated Sodom's sins.
Abraham? Perhaps Abraham had alerted Him.
More likely victims of the city's heavy, evil hand
Had cried for One to come and advocate for them.

Was it for the sake of economy
That Yahweh diverted His plan,
Adding an "unplanned" stop to His itinerary,
Pausing to rest in sight of Abraham's tent?

Or was it a part of His Divine economy
To enlist Abraham in the plan,
Add a priestly path to Abraham's itinerary,
And draw all nations to his tent?

See old Abraham run to fetch them bread,
To find at least some milk and curds.
Forgetting they had tasted angel fare
He rushed to feed them what he had.

The feast he set of fresh-baked bread,
Tender roasted lamb, of milk and curds,
Contrasted with the hurried tasteless fare
That Lot would serve from what he had.

Sensing, perhaps, a woman's touch
In the bread they ate, the men asked,
"Where is your wife, Sarah?"
"There in the tent," Abraham replied.

## Sandals: The Journey of Abraham and Sarah & Hagar

"In one year," said Yahweh, "because of my touch
Sarah will bear the son for which you asked."
"Why do you laugh, Sarah?"
"I did not laugh!" "You did!" He laughingly replied.

When the strangers rose to go their way
Abraham tagged along, allowed to hear
Them tell the purpose of their mission
And the part that he would play.

"Should I hide from Abraham the way
That he will bless all nations? Let him hear
The purpose of our mission.
He will know the part that he should play."

And so the deferential tone that Abraham employed,
Addressing Yahweh as *Adonai*, my Lord,
Served well his newly given role of mediator,
Pleading that a wayward nation might be saved.

It was not the first time Sodom had employed
Abraham's mediation, saving them and their lord.
But now, oblivious of their need of mediator,
They needed, more than ever, to be saved.

And Yahweh needed Abraham as well.
It is no small thing to rain down fire on a town.
One must have a reason, and clearly show
That justice had demanded such an act.

So Abraham served his God and Sodom well,
Revealing Yahweh's willingness to spare the town
If Abraham could clearly show
A righteous cause for Him to stay his awful act.

*Sandals: The Journey of Abraham and Sarah & Hagar*

    The Road To Zoar
      (Genesis 19)

The distance from the gates of Ur
To the mountains above Zoar
Is not measured in mere miles

Each signpost marks a turn
A yielding to some guiding star
Angelic light or demon's guile

From the heights above the plain
From the entrance of his cave
Old Lot surveyed his fateful path

Flight from Ur with hope of gain
Grasping of the best that Abram gave
A seat of honor at the gates of wrath

Snatched from raiders at Abram's risk
Saved from Sodom's fires by Abram's pleas
Escaped with skin and kin but barely so

And now before him children run and frisk
His double image in their face he sees
And ponders choices made so many miles ago

"I have two virgins here" he'd told the raging men
"The 'times' make them dispensable
Take them but leave my honored guests alone"

"We have no man but father" said the virgins as they lay with him
"The 'times' have made our deed more honorable"
So, in his drunken stupor, Lot knew nothing of the seeds he'd sown

And now he sees his sons, his grandsons, run and frisk
His double image in their face he sees
And ponders choices made so many miles ago

### Sandals: The Journey of Abraham and Sarah & Hagar

Sarai In Abimelech's Harem
(Genesis 12:10-20 & Genesis 20)

"Sarai, my sister–bride,
This is how you can show
Your love to me;
Everywhere we go, say of me,
'He is my brother.'
Then they'll let me live."

It was not a lie
That Abram asked of me;
A deception to be sure,
But not a lie.
A protection to ensure
That Abram would survive,
That Abram's offspring would endure.

Yahweh, Abram's God,
Did you know what Abram's plan
Would do to me?
Did you have a plan
To rescue me,
His "sister–bride",
From Pharaoh's harlotry;
Restore me to my place
And dignity?
Did Abram miss me,
Sleeping in his tent alone?
If I, a queen in Egypt, had become;
Had born, instead of Abram's seed,
A Pharaoh's son,
Would Abram then regret what he had done?
Would he – would You – would anyone
Remember Sarai's gift of love
To frightened Abram?

## Sandals: The Journey of Abraham and Sarah & Hagar

I should be thankful
That you rescued me.
I am thankful . . .
I never hoped to be
Anything but Abram's;
Abram's sister,
Abram's bride,
It mattered not to me.
But Abram's –
Wholly Abram's –
Is what I always longed to be.

And Abram's I was again
As we returned,
The wife of wealthy Abram,
Made rich by stealth and lie,
Made rich by Pharaoh's penance;
Another part of Abram's booty,
Carried along in triumph,
The generous gift
Of my Pharaoh–husband
To my brother–half
Along with the cattle and slaves,
The silver and gold
I had bought for him
With the lie I told.

And now, again,
I show my love for him
And save him from this Philistine
Whom Abram fears,
Becoming once again a "queen,"
A harem trophy for a stranger–king.
Yahweh, Abram's God!

*Sandals: The Journey of Abraham and Sarah & Hagar*

Is this the way you punish me
For laughing at your messenger?

Is this the way you plan for me
To bear a son,
Creating Abram's progeny?

Yahweh! Hear me!
To which Abram
Shall I show my love?
To him who leaves his settled home
And, fearless, goes
In search of one you've told him of,
Or to the one who, doubting,
Hides behind a lie,
And gives away his sister–bride
Each time he sees
A stranger drawing nigh?

Yahweh,
Have I shown sufficient love
That Abram,
Sleeping once again alone,
Is missing me?
I wonder, waiting here
Away from home,
If Abram has a plan to rescue me,
Or if, remembering,
He smiles and hopes
That once again,
Among the treasures he'll receive –
The sheep and cattle, and the gold –
Will be his wife
Whose love he's used again
To save his life.

*Sandals: The Journey of Abraham and Sarah & Hagar*

Abram, husband–half to me,
I've shown *my* love to you
Repeatedly,
And ever only asked
That I could be
The one who walks beside you
Constantly.
But now I sit alone again
And wonder if,
Or when,
Enfolded in *your* love,
I've ever been.

*Sandals: The Journey of Abraham and Sarah & Hagar*

    Unintended Consequences
(Abraham banishing Hagar and Ishmael)
        (Genesis 21:1-21)

Who could know that, from
    a simple "misdirection"
    all this grief could come?
It all started with a lie,
    a small deception.

"Say you are my sister," I said.
"I am his sister," she lied.
It seemed the right thing –
    the *providential* thing –
    to do.
Had not Yahweh given us
    this dual status?
And so we lied . . .
    I lied!
And now we come to this.

We laughed, the men and I,
    as we carted away
    the booty of Egypt –
    gold, cattle, grain,
    slaves, men, women
    and *children*.
    And Sarai.

Sarai rode, perched atop the stuff,
    not sharing our mirth,
    wearing royal silken scarves
        to hide rejection's scars,
    bitterly comparing royal courts
        with desert tarps.

*Sandals: The Journey of Abraham and Sarah & Hagar*

    Not sure anymore . . .

Queen? Sister? Wife?
    Despairing –
    despairing, most of all –
    of domestic life.

And so from among the booty
    she got a child,
      a girl, an Egyptian, Hagar,
    taken from her home, enslaved,
    made to roam, like her mistress, Sarai,
    bereft of hope for posterity.

Some sins are swift,
    demanding to be paid,
    destroying their minion
    in an instant.
Some lie hidden in the "stuff,"
    waiting, accruing interest,
    until their weight is
    great enough to crush.

"Go," Sarai said,
    her last hopes exhausted.
    "Sleep with my maidservant.
    Perhaps I can build a family
      through her."

It seemed the right thing –
    the *providential* thing –
    to do.
Hagar, gift of Egypt,
    barren servant girl,
    would bear

*Sandals: The Journey of Abraham and Sarah & Hagar*

    for barren Sarai
    a son, an heir,
    who'd bear the name of
    "Abram's son."
And so was born a son,
    God hears (Ishmael).
We rejoiced, Hagar and I.

The years confirmed our choice.
We watched him grow.
"He will be a wild donkey
    of a man." the angel said.

We laughed!
Our hearts delighted in him,
    his strength,
    his joy,
    his life.

Ishmael, "God hears."

God hears half–prayers,
    or prayers that are
        no prayers at all;
    hears, interprets
    Hagar's anguished, fearful cry,
    Sarai's bitter, doubting complaint;
    hears and knows and answers
    what the heart would pray.

When Yahweh answered Sarai's prayer
    He said,
    "From Sarah you will have a son."
I laughed,
    a silent laugh that hid my doubts:
    "From a man a hundred years old?"

*Sandals: The Journey of Abraham and Sarah & Hagar*

"From a woman ninety?"
Aloud I said,
    "Hear me Lord!
    If only Ishmael might live under
        your blessing!"

"I heard you speak.
    Ishmael, son of *your* doing,
        will father twelve nations;
    Hagar's son's will be
        too numerous to count."

"I heard as well, your silent, bitter,
    doubting laugh.
Sarah *will* bear a son
    *of My doing*
    and you will call him
    Laughter (Isaac).

Through Isaac I will laugh
    at your deceits,
    at your lie–bought gains,
    at your presumptuous plans.
It is with Isaac
    I will make my covenant."

And so Sarah's son, my son,
    was born . . .
    and we come to this:

"Get rid of that slave woman,"
Sarah said, "and her son!
Her son will never share
in the inheritance with my son, Isaac."

## Sandals: The Journey of Abraham and Sarah & Hagar

"Lord Yahweh," I cried,
    "this cannot be!
    Ishmael is *my* son!"

"But he is not *My* son, Abraham.
Ishmael is *your* son, the son
    of *your* deceptions,
    the son of *your* making.
    For your sake,
        because he is *your* descendent,
        I will make him a great nation.

But Isaac is *My* son,
    the son of the promise
    I made to you in Ur.
Through him your *seed*
    will be counted.
Do as Sarah says
    and send the boy away."

And so the lie has accrued full weight.
The water skins and bread
    I lay on Hagar's shoulders,
    made heavy by my care for them,
        as heavy as her strength can bear,
    are light compared to what
        our grieving hearts must bear.

Who could know that, from
    a simple "misdirection"
    all this grief could come?
It started with a lie,
    a small deception,
    and where it ends
    I cannot see.

*Sandals: The Journey of Abraham and Sarah & Hagar*

The Voice of God
(Sarai Musing)

How does Yahweh speak?
What voice does He use?
Does He speak to all
But only some can hear?

Abram says he hears God speak,
That he is sure – and he can quote,
Word for word, with specificity,
The things God says to him.

A man appears who looks,
To every other eye,
Like any other man,
But Abram sees his God.

A cloud mounts up,
And thunder claps,
And in the cloud, and in the sound,
He sees and hears His God.

In sleep he dreams,
And waking, knows the dream
Was not a dream at all;
The Angel of the Lord had come.

A sadness, or a joy,
It matters not;
Each mood is fraught
With words of God for him.

*Sandals: The Journey of Abraham and Sarah & Hagar*

A thought, a simple thought,
That in another mind
Would fly as soon as it was thought,
To Abram, is the voice of God.

How does Yahweh speak?
What voice does He use?
Does He speak to all
But only some can hear?

Abram shapes his life
By what he "hears",
And shapes the lives of others;
Shapes ten thousand, thousand
    lives to come.

*Sandals: The Journey of Abraham and Sarah & Hagar*

    On the Mountain
    (Genesis 22)

The steep way bites into the feet
    of the young man carrying the wood;
    stings the lungs of the old man
    carrying the fire and the knife.

Evasive answers meet their questions;
    "Father, where is the sacrifice?"
    "Yahweh, where *is* the sacrifice?"
    Faith alone bears them to their doom.

The old man, famous for his faith,
    leads his trusting son, bearing,
    bound to his strong back,
    the wood for his own immolation.

A crude stone altar rises;
    stone on stone,
    the old man's calloused hands
    place each with practiced certainty.

The wood is laid,
    enough to consume the offering;
    the young man, bound, knows now,
    the dreadful answer to his question.

The old man, famous for his faith,
    lays his trusting son upon the wood;
    his son, his only son, the one he loves, is,
    he knows, the answer to his question.

*Sandals: The Journey of Abraham and Sarah & Hagar*

The knife is raised, glinting in the sun,
    an everlasting symbol
    of the old man's faithful willingness
    to sacrifice his only son.

And Yahweh, Yahweh who speaks only to command,
    never to explain, watches all,
    and knows the sorrow of the father,
        the terror of the son.

He sees another hill, another Father,
    famous for his love,
    who gives his son, his only son, the one he loves,
    to be the answer to The Question.

*Sandals: The Journey of Abraham and Sarah & Hagar*

At Kiriath Arba
(Genesis 23:1)

The years, at last, had left her plain;
Stole the beauty that had made her queen
Of every sphere she entered,
Crowned her queen in three kingdoms.

The years had taken more, alas;
Had robbed the joy of childhood love
And left a hollow, bitter shell
That echoed with her pain.

The years of longing, filled with tears,
Broken briefly with a single joy,
Returned with vengeance to anoint
Her final lonely days.

And now, now this awful news!
Not surprising; nothing is surprising
To one who has lived with one whose sole desire
Is to be a friend of Yahweh God.

Years she'd had to reminisce, recalling
Happy days in Ur, brought to an unhappy end
By Yahweh's call to leave that home
For years of homeless wandering.

Years – four score and ten –
That robbed her of all hope;
That made her laugh at anyone
Who dared to offered hope to her.

Wealth! Ah there was wealth.
Wealth enough that she could stay
And watch the servants tend the flocks

*Sandals: The Journey of Abraham and Sarah & Hagar*

While he went off to hear from God.

And worse, the only joy she'd ever known,
The only laughter in her life, he stripped away.
At Beer Lahai Roi, that storied well that kept alive
The Egyptian and her unborn son, he kept her son.

And news came back to taunt her heart,
Of sons and daughters, born to the Egyptian's hateful son;
Grandsons and granddaughters of her former maid.
Was it for them he stayed at Beer Lahai Roi?

She had seen the little band pass by,
One donkey and a few men headed north.
The thought had come, though little hope,
That it might, at last, be them.

And now, now this awful news!
She'd always known that nothing Abram owned
Was kept from Yahweh's claims;
Not home, or wealth, or life itself.

But this was more than heart or mind could bear.
Would Yahweh ask him for his – for her – only son?
If Isaac had not born the news to her
It would have seemed a horrid dream.

"This is how you can show that you love me. . ."
She remembered Abram's words, and they stuck in her throat,
Burned in her mind, erased all love she had for him.
She wondered, had Yahweh said those words to him?

And so, these final years she lived and died alone,
Long miles from Abraham at Beer Lahai Roi,
Farther still from Isaac at Beer Sheba,
All laughter, joy, and beauty, faded by the years.

*Sandals: The Journey of Abraham and Sarah & Hagar*

An Old Woman Remembers
   (Hagar's Recompense)

See them coming from the desert,
A prize of faces, a clamor of voices,
A march of legs and arms
Too numerous to count;

Brought alive, by the hunter,
Trophies from the wilderness,
Untamed and untamable,
Beautiful before my eyes.

> In a barren land we wept;
> You heard the cry of the lad,
> Saw my tears,
> Felt his father's grief.
>
> "Call him Ishmael", you said,
> "For I have heard his cry;
> At Beer Lahai Roi
> I saw your plight."
>
> "A wild man he will be
> With bowstring drawn;
> His hand against all;
> Against him, all hands."
>
> "Twelve nations!
> Sons, and sons of sons,
> Gracing your aged head,
> Gladdening his father's heart."

*Sandals: The Journey of Abraham and Sarah & Hagar*

See them come, El Roi?
Children of the wilderness,
Wild men, and glad,
Strong men, well–fed.

Bearing nations in their loins,
Children of Abraham,
Offspring of the outcast,
Inhabiting, inheriting the land.

*Sandals: The Journey of Abraham and Sarah & Hagar*

Abraham At Sarah's Tomb
(Genesis 23)

Sarai, sister–bride, may I at last, talk to you?
We used to talk . . . and laugh,
Remembering the prankish things you'd do
To your older brother–half.

But as the years wore on, the talking ceased.
Your laughter lost its joy, became a scoff,
A sneer, a way to wound, a dis–belief,
A lash you used to drive me off.

I knew no joy to supercede
The hours I watched your childhood play.
Anything that you could ask or need,
I'd fetch and bring you right away.

And as you grew, you followed all my ways;
My little *Underfoot,* you came to be,
Gladly fetching things for me on busy days,
Suffering wounded feet which I inflicted thoughtlessly.

Oh, Sarah! I know my ways have wounded you.
How I have wished, each time I turned and broke your heart,
That there could be another way, Yahweh's will to do;
Another way that would not drive our hearts apart.

Oh Yahweh! Have I done her ill; used Your Name in vain;
Said You *said,* when it was only I who *thought* a thing?
Have I sacrificed a love, and done it in Your Name;
Made, "Yahweh said," with hollow terror ring?

Sister–bride, when did love begin to die?
Was it when I took you from the gilded streets of Ur?

*Sandals: The Journey of Abraham and Sarah & Hagar*

Or was it that I ask that you would love me through a lie,
Demoting you from wife to pawn, *my* safety to ensure?

Did the love of Ishmael, and yes, of Hagar too,
Drive a wedge between our hearts?
Did my grieving at their plight seem to you
A theft of love that should have been your part?

Yahweh, my sins have grown like desert weeds
That thrive in drought and heat,
Producing thorns, and *more* weed seeds;
*More* bitter fruit unfit to eat.

Sarai, once an infant–in–my–arms,
Half an arm's length at the start,
But gaining, yearly, woman's charms,
Until your beauties filled my heart.

Sarai, lovely desert rose,
Beauty graced you, head to toes,
And beauty graced the day you chose,
Your life, with mine, to juxtapose.

To juxtapose! A term, fitting, I suppose;
Never quite together, never really one,
Half–sister, half–wife, part real, part pose,
Two hearts half–given, but never fully won.

Yahweh, did You think that You could win
Her heart, through me, as You won mine,
But never speak to her to let her in?
"In hope of Abram's hope," her faith defined.

Faith, defined in hope of hope, is thin;
Too thin to stand the test and stress of time.

*Sandals: The Journey of Abraham and Sarah & Hagar*

Sandals bought in Ur will fail when
Walking paths that You, Almighty God, define.

Sarah, about Isaac I need to say some things.
The barren years had turned your joy to bitter pain.
But when his laughter came it made you whole again;
Your joy deferred, came, long last, like dancing rain.

How do I tell you your love for him was wrong;
That any love that overtops the love of God
Invites a test to see if we are strong
Enough to bow beneath His rod?

Yahweh knew my heart, and Isaac's too;
It was not for us alone He made the test.
He needed, just as much, to see if you
Would give to him your earthly best.

You wept to see the gods of Ur reduced to dust,
And thought me cruel when I crushed them 'neath my hand.
But then you shaped another god and put, in him, your trust.
So Yahweh called on me, again, to slay your god beneath my hand.

Forgive her, Yahweh; take her in.
Give her joys she never had in life.
Forgive me, Yahweh, for my sins.
And thank you for Sarah, my sister–wife.

*Sandals: The Journey of Abraham and Sarah & Hagar*

The Burial of Abraham
(Genesis 25:1-10)

The procession moved slowly
Guided by the old men
Leaning heavily upon their staves
No words passed between them

Their silence born not wholly
Of fatigue, broken only when
The elder brother gave
The sign to stop, or start again

Separated almost on the day
Of the younger brother's birth
They had never shared the feast
That feeds a dialogue

All the mothers' tales that they
Were fed served only to add girth
To their bloated biases, increased
Resentment's cherished catalog

But he was father to them both,
Grandfather to Ishmael's
Swelling clans
To Isaac's youthful sons

And so, as though an oath
Had drawn against their will,
The winding caravans
Climbed toward the setting sun.

*Sandals: The Journey of Abraham and Sarah & Hagar*

Ishmael waved his sons
To open up the tomb
Isaac's twins stood by
Young Jacob, young Esau

Did Ishmael flinch upon
The sight within the gloom
Of bones? And did he try
To hide the tightness in his jaw?

With Abraham laid to rest
Beside the bones in Sarah's grave
An era ended and
The Tomb was sealed again

The old men halted at the crest
Rested on their staves
Considered offering a hand
Turned instead and nodded to their waiting bands

*Sandals: The Journey of Abraham and Sarah & Hagar*

A Complicated Faith

When we are told
That Abram had great faith
It does not mean he had it all the time
Or most of the time
Or even that he had it often.

We see his faith appear to waver
When he stops in Haran,
Awaiting Terah's death,
Instead of going to the land
That Yahweh told him of.

We see him doubt
The power of God
To meet his needs
In famine stricken Canaan;
Running off instead to Egypt.

And there his doubts –
His fears – inspire a lie
That haunts his steps
For all his life
And all his children's lives to come.

He yields to Sarai's doubt
And taking Hagar
Bears a son
Whom he could never
Fully call his own.

*Sandals: The Journey of Abraham and Sarah & Hagar*

He laughed in doubt
When told that he, at ninety-nine,
And Sarah ten years younger,
Would have a child
Just one year hence.

And once again his doubt –
His fear of Abimelech –
Compelled a lie
And cast a shadow
On the birth of Isaac.

So, when we are told
That Abram had great faith
It does not mean he had it all the time
Or most of the time,
Or even that he had it often.

It means instead that Abram
Was a God-ward man – imperfect.
But when he stumbled
It was not for lack of want,
But lack of light to find his way.

Abram was an *Underfoot*,
He followed close to God,
Eyes upon him, ears attuned,
And heart determined
Not to miss a turn He made.

*Sandals: The Journey of Abraham and Sarah & Hagar*

    A One Way Conversation With God
        (Poet's Privilege)

I'm confused, God!
You're not surprised.
In your patience you've endured
A lifetime of my confusion,
My questions, my doubt,
My foolish surmising,
My impetuous conjectures.

Grant me, once again,
The chance – I have no right –
To question you.

I see old Abram packing up,
Preparing to leave an established home,
With no thought of a return,
Heading to a land that you would "show him."
Confident, he seems, that you have spoken;
Prepared, he is, to wander
In a land he can't possess.

I read that you *spoke* to him,
*Told* him to leave his home,
*Said* that you would *show* him where to go.

What am I to make of these words:
*Spoke – told – said – show?*
What am I to make of his response:
He *left* his home,
*Took all* he had,
*Set out* for Canaan,
*Arrived* there and worshiped you.

*Sandals: The Journey of Abraham and Sarah & Hagar*

Lord, I want to *hear* you speak,
And *know*, with the certainty of Abram,
That I've *heard* your voice.

Can I assume that you are always near me,
Always speaking?
Is it that I have ears, adequate to hear,
But am not hearing;
That I have eyes, adequate to see,
But am not seeing;
A heart that could, but will not perceive you?

What advantage did Abram have
That I am denied?
None, as far as I can see.

He was not required to see,
In the face of a stranger,
The face of his God.
But Abram saw you in the midst
Of ordinary things, believed you,
And you credited that to him
As righteousness.

Lord, may I assume without presumption,
That all I see, and hear, and read, and think;
That all I'm shown and taught;
That every face and form, every sight and sound,
Every sorrow, and every joy,
Bears to me a chance to hear your voice;
That Abram's God is always near,
        and wants to speak to me?

*Sandals: The Journey of Abraham and Sarah & Hagar*

*Sandals: The Journey of Abraham and Sarah & Hagar*

Afterword

Themes in the Early Prosaic and Poetic Texts of the Hebrew Bible

*Whenever your son shall ask you later, saying, "To what pertains the testimonies and the statutes and the ordinances which YHWH our God has commanded you?" Then you shall say to your son, "Slaves we were to Pharaoh in Egypt; and YHWH brought us from Egypt with a mighty hand; . . . and us He brought from there, that He might bring us to give to us the land which He promised to our fathers. (Deuteronomy 6:20-21, 23)*

*(Note: Biblical quotations are the author's translations from the Hebrew.)*

Religion as understood generally by human individuals, and as given expression by their communities, can be stated to be the total response of the total human personality to that which is apprehended as ultimate reality. This responsive experience is the most intense of which the human is capable, and this responsive experience impels the human to act – often, but not exclusively, in literary modes, and equally frequently reflective of human participation within community.

Already early in the twentieth century, we were made aware by a plethora of studies that the ancient Hebrew mind, like much of its environment, gave expression to this responsiveness in the form of its early poetry – a poetry expressed within the peculiarities of its linguistic necessities and scattered throughout what we now possess as a series of prose books. Most notable among these ancient poems, which take us back to the origins both of a people and of their relationship to their God, are such impressive examples as Genesis 49:1-27; Exodus 15:1-18; Numbers 21:14-15, 17-18, 27-29; 23:7-10, 18-24; 24:3-9, 15-24; Deuteronomy 32:1-43; 33:2-29; Judges 5:2-31. Among these, beside their illustration of Hebrew poetic form, are a few

*Sandals: The Journey of Abraham and Sarah & Hagar*

infrequent indications of the kind of sources in which they were initially incorporated and from which they were brought into these later prose contexts, most notable examples being Numbers 21:14 "Book of the Wars of YHWH"; Numbers 21:27 "the balladers sing".

In addition to old poetry, liturgical requirements for a continuing response find expression somewhat more prosaically, though also illustrative of Hebrew cadence. These appear sequentially, yet almost developmentally, as one progresses through the historical changes of Hebrew temporal life, beginning already with reference to the initial coming "into the land which YHWH your God gives you for an inheritance" (Deuteronomy 26:5-10), and then as expanded so as to incorporate the subsequent history, made each time fuller and more specific, as found in Joshua 24:2-13; 1 Samuel 12:8-13; Nehemiah 9:6-37. Moreover, specific psalms combine this historical confession into a more poetic form, often picking up and elaborating upon poetic fragments scattered in the prose narratives: for example Psalm 68 developing Numbers 10:25 and echoing Judges 5. Fuller poetic renderings of the redeeming act of deliverance of this people by their God are found in Psalm 44, 105, 106, 114, 135, 136 – to name but a few, yet indicative of the capacity to play off of the basic historical themes.

Looking back again to Deuteronomy 26:5-10, one immediately ascertains that among those fundamental themes are included:

1) the "wandering Aramaean" as basic father of these tribes;
2) the "going down into Egypt" and "sojourning there, few in number";
3) The increase into a nation of greater proportions;
4) the oppressive treatment by the Egyptians;
5) the "crying out to YHWH the God of our fathers";
6) the deliverance from Egypt by this YHWH;
7) the "bringing us into this place – a land flowing with milk and honey".

*Sandals: The Journey of Abraham and Sarah & Hagar*

When we read the larger text, from Genesis through Joshua, in the total Hebrew Bible as now gathered (and as already gathered well before the outset of the Christian or Common Era – in fact, clearly gathered as the larger narrative clear up to the Exile into Babylon accompanying the initial destruction of Jerusalem by the Babylonians after 586 BCE), what we become aware of is how the ordering of that narrative fills out and makes explicit those personalities and events which constitute the basic understanding of this specific human history under the covenanted relationship with this specific deity – a story that begins rather abruptly after lengthy sequences of genealogical succession (in Genesis 5 plus 11:10-32):

> *Now YHWH said to Abram, "Go from your country and your kindred and the house of your father to the land which I will show you." (Genesis 12:1)*

The enlarged version of *"the wandering Aramaean" theme* begins specifically from Haran (Genesis 11:31) in the region of the Upper Euphrates designated Aram Naharaim (literally Aram "of the two rivers", namely the Euphrates and its major tributary, the Habur, hence translated into Greek and subsequently by "Mesopotamia": Genesis 24:10) or Paddan Aram (the "broad plans" between rivers: Genesis 25:20 etc.), and sets forth into the land of Canaan, which anticipate *the final theme*. The linguistic distinction between Aramaic and Canaanite remains evident later on in the naming of a "heap of stones" marking a boundary between descendent kin (Genesis 32:44-49). Once settled into "the land", "the lip/tongue of Canaan" comes to prevail as spoken language of these folk (Isaiah 19:18), such that their Aramaen heritage is preserved almost exclusively in these narratives of those ancestral migrators responding to the divine initiative. While individuals among them can be designated as "Hebrew" (Genesis 14:13 of Abram himself), that term is never used with respect to language within the Hebrew Bible, but only comes in with the later traditions including Sirach (prologue 22) or Acts (21:40). As the Judaean monarchy of

*Sandals: The Journey of Abraham and Sarah & Hagar*

David and his successors prevails, so does the tendency to designate the common language as that "of Judah". For a primary illustration of contrasting sentiments with regard to these languages, note the historical account given in 2 Kings 18:13-37, especially at verses 26 and 28. The stories in Genesis of the successive descendent situations continuing *this theme*, applied to Isaac and Jacob/Israel, bear out the connection to the Aramaic homelands by the necessity of returning there for wives of these heirs within the originating tribal clan (respectively, Genesis 24, obtaining Rebekah for Isaac, Genesis 28-31, achieving Leah and Rachel for and by Jacob).

> *Now there was a famine in the land. So Abram went down to Egypt to sojourn there, for the famine was heavy in the land. (Genesis 12:10)*

The *second and fourth themes* developed reflect the consequences relative to agricultural possibilities – both those of animal husbandry as well as direct grain production. The new land of Canaan, like the more ancient homeland of Aram, depended upon "rain water", while the regions further to the East and South, including the valleys of the Tigris and the Euphrates, produced abundant crops and herds with the cooperation of irrigation-managed, rain-nourished river water, subject however to the risk of excess from mountain run-off and a tradition of great floods. On the other hand, the region to the more immediate South, but into the continent of Africa, namely the valley of the Nile, demonstrated normally what a more dependable source, beyond the knowledge of those times, could be depended upon to produce from annual inundations carefully managed (a situation well-described within the interpretative dreams of the larger story of Joseph, in Genesis 37 and 39-41). The trade-off for food-stuffs is some level of oppression, which begins to appear immediately (Genesis 12:10-20) with *the sub-theme "threat to the ancestress"* without whom the fulfillment of the promise of "descendents as the dust of the earth" (Genesis 13:16) could not be attained. That oppressive situation is reiterated (again for Sarai/Sarah, Abram's sister-wife, so Genesis

*Sandals: The Journey of Abraham and Sarah & Hagar*

20:12), in Genesis 20 though the setting is not all the way into Egypt; and newly for Isaac's wife in Genesis 29 where the setting is nearer Egypt in what had become the land of the Philistines about 1200 BCE. To *the sub-theme of attaining wives for the sons*, adjacent concerns arise: 1) to that wife's capacity to bear a child, and the consequences when it is not easily attained, and 2) to conflict among children already in the womb or to conflict among wives by the number and diversity of their children. The narratives (Genesis 17 of Isaac's twins) or poetic fragments (Genesis 49 of Jacob's twelve) of blessing bear each of the latter out. Related, but of another order of complexity, is the human issue by the alternate wife, another kind of "threat to the ancestress" (primarily Ishmael by Hagar in Genesis 16:1-16; 21:9-21; but observe also those by Keturah after Sarah's death in Genesis 25:1-6, as well as the several maid servants respectively of Leah and Rachel by whom Jacob bore additional children, according to Genesis 29:31-30:24, whose repercussions dominate the old blessing poetry in Genesis 49:2-17). The Ishmael narrative becomes the more abiding example of consequence due to the rise of Islam in the seventh century CE with its own literary significance for the Qu'ran!

> *The God <ha-Elohim, not YHWY!> said <to Abraham>,*
> *"Take your son, your only son whom you love, even Isaac,*
> *and go to the land of Moriah, and offer him there as a burnt*
> *offering upon one of the mountains of which I shall tell unto*
> *you." (Genesis 22:2)*

The *third theme* is a consequence of the various elements of the *second theme*, both the needs to move southward from Canaan proper into Egypt and its intermediate areas of the Negeb or of the Philistines. Such matters, of course, do not cease by the end of Genesis, and their larger fruition requires much of the narrative portions of Exodus, Numbers, and Joshua (with attention given also to Deuteronomy 1-3). However, the greater *theme of growth* is mitigated by another kind of *sub-theme threat*, this time to the only, or primary, or the significantly-designated son and heir, illustrated at its most intensive by the peculiar

## Sandals: The Journey of Abraham and Sarah & Hagar

testing in a mode reminiscent of the remnant of human sacrifice (Genesis 22:1-19). One might well note how the sharp focus of this account has come to significance in the modern world, be that of the secularizing problems of Europe already during the 19th century in the written thought of Soren Kierkegaard, or in the post-Holocaust agonies of the second half of the 20th century in the written thought of Emmanuel Levinas!

> ... *a word of YHWH was to Abram in a vision, Fear not, Abram, I <am> your shield." (Genesis 15:1)*

The *fifth and sixth themes* take us into the heart of the religious elements. The deity of action and deliverance has a most peculiar name! But the antiquity of those developed narratives which give fullness to the overarching integration of these diverse themes recall an era of some considerable remoteness when both the names of those who respond and "that ultimate reality" to which they respond could still be designated by a diversity of modes of identification, which diversity was neither, nor could it have been, smoothed out by the final bringing together of the Traditions in which such were embedded.

When the descendents of father Abram are initially settled into the promised land of Canaan, a fuller version (Joshua 24:2-13) of the responsive recitation details much more than the earlier form previously met (Deuteronomy 26:5-10). At its conclusion there is placed before the people, the necessity for a choice involving the alternative deities which might be served. Our observation of these alternatives (Joshua 24:14-15, 17) provide an appropriate prelude to the consideration of the deity involved in the call to Abram:

1) the gods your fathers served in the region "beyond *the* River";
2) the gods your fathers served in Egypt;
3) the gods of the Amorites in whose land you dwell;
4) YHWH, who brought us and our fathers up from the land of Egypt.

*Sandals: The Journey of Abraham and Sarah & Hagar*

While these alternatives can be more poetically described negatively (Deuteronomy 32:15-18), there is no hint that the choosing lacked real significance. Rather one finds that the alternatives posed are parallel to the responsive recitation, with these nuances of localization employed: Aram Haharaim is now perceived from the more western perspective as the eastern region "beyond *the* River" <=Euphrates>, while the reference to the "land of Canaan" reflects the principal inhabitants from the pre-monarchical era as "Amorites" (those of Amurru land), identified in other ancient Near Eastern sources as the "westerners" who live, from a more eastern perspective, "beyond the river" Euphrates westward toward "the Great Sea" <=Mediterranean; Numbers 34:6> and southward toward Egypt. Various combinations of the inhabitants will get enumerated:

> *On that day YHWH cut a covenant with Abram, saying "To your descendents I give this land, from the river of Egypt up to the great river, the river Euphrates: that of the Qenites, and the Qenizzites, and the Qadmonites, and Hittites, and the Perizzites, and the Rephaim, and the Amorites, and the Canaanites, and Girgashites, and the Jebusites." (Genesis 15:18-21)*

But the people will also be reminded at a much later date: "Your origin and your birth are of the land of the Canaanites; your father was an Amorite, and your mother a Hittite" (Ezekiel 16:2 in one of the greater metaphorical descriptions coming from the era of destruction and exile).

Clearly, settle land and its economic commodities are the underlying realities which make tempting the alternative choices! And while the choice which prevailed literarily reflects a developmental history posed as basic from these origins within the fulfilled promise which accompanied the deliverance from the oppressive burden of slavery in Egypt, nevertheless, the ancient accounts of the ancestral fathers

## Sandals: The Journey of Abraham and Sarah & Hagar

preserves remnants of a much older situation. As was noted more than eighty years ago (Alt 1929; English translation 1968:32), "It is the rarest of the titles of the God of the Fathers that give the impression of the greatest antiquity." Hence we meet, along with "the God of Abraham", "the fear of Isaac" (Genesis 31:42), and "the Mighty One of Jacob" (Genesis 49:24, with interpretative gloss "the name of the Shepherd, the Rock of Israel"), or "God Most High" (Genesis 14:18-20,22) and "God Almighty" (Genesis 17:1).

What becomes noteworthy then, when "a word of YHWH was to Abram in a vision" (Genesis 15:1), is not merely the analogous construction "the Shield of Abram", but the grammatical affirmation in Hebrew that "I" is that "shield", where "adonai <'my Lord'> YHWH" is He unto whom Abram has pledged, renews pledging, and affirms ever after his covenanted pledge of faithfulness. In as clear an etymology as Scripture ever allows, in the subsequent era of Mosaic narrative, the "I" of YHWH will be elaborated to define as meaning of YHWH, and stated from a perspective internal to the deity: "'HYH asher 'HYH" – employing thereby the first person singular, of the Hebrew root HY/WH, to provide understanding of the third person singular of the same root (YHWH) as personal name for that same God in the very moment of the deliverance from Egypt (Exodus 3:13-22, especially at verse 14).

It is out from these kinds of "odd, hidden, dense, and inscrutable dimensions" (Brueggemann 1997:104, 105) which one confronts in materials from some three millennia past, that our contemporary poet has chosen to give focus to "Abraham and Sarah" by this "Suite of Poems". Herein lies a profound meditation upon aspects of the text of Genesis duly composed within a celebrative Tradition, brilliantly conceived and executed, whose crucial ingredient, lying beneath the primary patriarchal (and its most necessary accompanying matriarchal) account, remains that of the legitimate tension between "faith and doubt" so highly evident even in one of whom the text had reason to

*Sandals: The Journey of Abraham and Sarah & Hagar*

affirm that "he believed in YHWH, and He reckoned it to him as righteousness" (Genesis 15:6).

Clyde Curry Smith
4 July 2010

*Sandals: The Journey of Abraham and Sarah & Hagar*

SELECTED BIBLIOGRAPHY

Alt, Albrecht. 1929. ***Der Gott der Väter,*** "Beiträge zur Wissenschaft vom Alten un Neuen Testament", III Folge, Heft 12; translated as "the God of the Fathers", by R. A. Wilson, in ***Essay on Old Testament History and Religion.*** Garden City, NY: Doubleday Anchor Books, 1968; pp. 3-100.

Bentzen, Aage. 1957. "Profane and Religious Poetry", in ***Introduction to the Old Testament,*** Volume I. Copenhagen: B.E.C. Gad Publisher; pp. 122-167.

Brueggemann, Walter. 1997. ***Theology of the Old Testament:*** Testimony, Dispute, Advocacy. Minneapolis, MN: Fortress Press.

Gervirtz, Stanley. 1963. ***Patterns in the Early Poetry of Israel.*** "Studies in Ancient Oriental Civilizations", No. 32. Chicago, IL: The Oriental Institute of the University of Chicago.

Kierkegaard, Soren Asbye. 1843. ***Fear and Trembling;*** translated with Introduction and Notes, by Walter Lowrie, in ***Fear and Trembling and The Sickness Unto Death.*** Garden City, NY: Doubleday Anchor Books, 1954; pp. 21-132.

Levinas, Emmanuel. 1996. "Kierkegaard: Existence and Ethics" in ***Proper Names.*** Palo Alto, CA: Stanford University Press; chapter 8, pp. 66-74.

Noth, Martin. 1928. ***Die israelitischen Personennname im Rahmen der gemeinsemitischen Namegebung.*** "Beiträge zur Wissenschaft vom Alten un Neuen Testament", III Folge, Heft 10. Stuttgart: W. Kohlhammer.

*Sandals: The Journey of Abraham and Sarah & Hagar*

Oesterley, W. O. E. 1938. *Ancient Hebrew Poems*: Metrically Translated with Introductions and Notes. London: Society for Promoting Christian Knowledge.

Poeble, Arno. 1932. "Das appositionell bestimmte Pronomen der 1. pers. Sing. in den westseitischen Inschriften und im alten Testament", *Assyriological Studies*, No. 3 Chicago, IL: The Oriental Institute of the University of Chicago.

Smith, Clyde Curry. 1990. "Joachim Wach", in *Great lives from History: Twentieth Century*, Volume V, edited by Frank N. Magill. Pasadena, CA: Salem Press; pp. 2384-2389.

Smith George Adam. 1912. *The early Poetry of Israel in its Physical and Social Origins*. "The Schweich Lectures 1910". London; Published for the British Academy.

von Rad, Gerhard. 1938. *Das forgeschichteliche Problem des Hexateuch*. Stuttgart: W. Kohlhammer; translated as *The Problem of the Hexateuch and other Essays*, by E. W. Trueman Dicken. Edinburgh and London: Oliver & Boyd, 1966.

von Rad, Gerhard. 1961. *Genesis: A Commentary*, translated by John H. Marks, "The Old Testament Library". London: SCM Press Ltd.

von Rad, Gerhard. 1962. *Old Testament Theology*, Volume I: The theology of Israel's Historical Traditions, translated by D.M.G. Stalker. New York: Harper & Brothers.

Wach, Joachim. 1951. "Universals in Religion" in *Types of Religious Experience, Christian and Non-Christian*. Chicago, IL: The University of Chicago Press; pp. 30-37.

*Sandals: The Journey of Abraham and Sarah & Hagar*

*Sandals: The Journey of Abraham and Sarah & Hagar*

## Alphabetical Listing of Poems

| | |
|---|---|
| A Complicated Faith | 60 |
| A One-way Conversation With God | 62 |
| A Well Planned Encounter | 34 |
| Abraham at Sarah's Tomb | 55 |
| Abram's Decision | 11 |
| After the Rescue of Lot | 29 |
| An Old Woman Remembers (Hagar's Recompense) | 53 |
| At Kiriath Arba | 51 |
| Changes | 5 |
| Circumcision | 33 |
| Hagar On The Run | 32 |
| Looking Two Ways | 18 |
| Maiden Prayer | 9 |
| Melchizedek | 27 |
| On The Mountain | 49 |
| Revelation | 7 |
| Sandals | 3 |
| Sarai In A New Land | 20 |
| Sarai In Abimelech's Harem | 38 |
| Sarai | 1 |
| Sarai's Decision | 14 |
| Sarai's Wedding Day | 16 |
| Springtime | 24 |
| The Altars of Abraham | 25 |
| The Burial of Abraham | 58 |
| The First Quarrel | 22 |
| The Proposal | 13 |
| The Road To Zoar | 37 |
| The Voice of God | 47 |
| Underfoot | 2 |
| Unintended Consequences | 42 |

*Sandals: The Journey of Abraham and Sarah & Hagar*

*Sandals: The Journey of Abraham and Sarah & Hagar*

## About The Author

James (Jim) Rapp is a retired public school teacher.

Previous to his 27 year teaching career he served as pastor of a congregation in River Falls, Wisconsin for six years. In the years since his retirement from teaching he served his church in Eau Claire, Wisconsin as Director of Drama for 12 years until May 2009.

Jim holds a Diploma in Theology from North Central Bible College (now North Central University) 1958, and a Master's Degree in History from University of Wisconsin-River Falls 1971, with his major area of interest being the Ancient Near East.

He has written seven dramas, five of which have been staged. In his twelve years as Director of Drama he co-directed, with Music Director, Cheryl Brandt, twenty-two adult musical dramas and nine children's musicals.

Jim is author of three additional books of poetry, *Perfect Imperfection, Second Crop: More Poems by James D. Rapp*, and *Etcetera: An Eclectic expression of Humors*.

He is also author of *Inga & Olaf: Modern Parables* and *Sermon on the Mount: Brief Meditations*.

Jim lives with Alice, his wife of 56 plus years, in Eau Claire, Wisconsin.

*Sandals: The Journey of Abraham and Sarah & Hagar*

www.ingramcontent.com/pod-product-compliance
Lightning Source LLC
Chambersburg PA
CBHW071317040426
42444CB00009B/2033